KING JOHN
AND
MAGNA CARTA

PITKIN

IMPORTANT DATES

BAD KING JOHN:
KING OF ENGLAND 1199–1216

'HE FEARED NOT GOD, NOR RESPECTED MEN.'
Gerald of Wales

—

'A PILLAGER OF HIS OWN PEOPLE.'
The Barnwell annalist

—

N O king in English history has such a terrible reputation as 'Bad' King John. Other kings were as incompetent (Edward II), or perhaps as cruel (Richard III), but in the eyes of his contemporaries John seems to have been uniquely both. Here we tell the story of John and how his disastrous and bloody reign led to one of the most famous documents in history: Magna Carta.

A 12th-century fresco depicting King John with Isabella of Angoulême and Eleanor of Aquitaine.

PRINCe JOhN

JOHN was born in Oxford on Christmas Eve 1167. His father was the great Henry II and his mother the redoubtable Eleanor of Aquitaine, one of England's most famous queens. John was their lastborn of four surviving sons and was never expected to be king. Although he seemed to live in the shadow of his older brothers – Henry, Geoffrey and the illustrious Richard the Lionheart – he was his father's favourite. Henry indulged John, yet John was to repay him with treachery. As the youngest, John felt that he did not have ownership of as much territory from his father's Angevin Empire in England, Ireland and France that he felt he deserved; hence he was known as 'Lackland'.

Even as a young man and prince of the realm, John displayed some of the characteristics and tendencies that were to make him so notorious in later life. In 1185 in his role as Lord of Ireland (held since the age of 12), John visited the country. Here he squandered his money and offended the Irish lords by mocking their unfashionably long beards. Then in 1189, at the end of a long reign, his father King Henry II is said to have died from a broken heart when he learned that his beloved John had sided with the rebellion against him.

King Henry II, John's father (r.1154–89).

Opposite: Map of the dominions of the Angevins, c.1170 The Angevin Empire describes the collection of states (in Ireland, England and France) ruled by the Angevin dynasty (namely Henry II, Richard the Lionheart and King John).

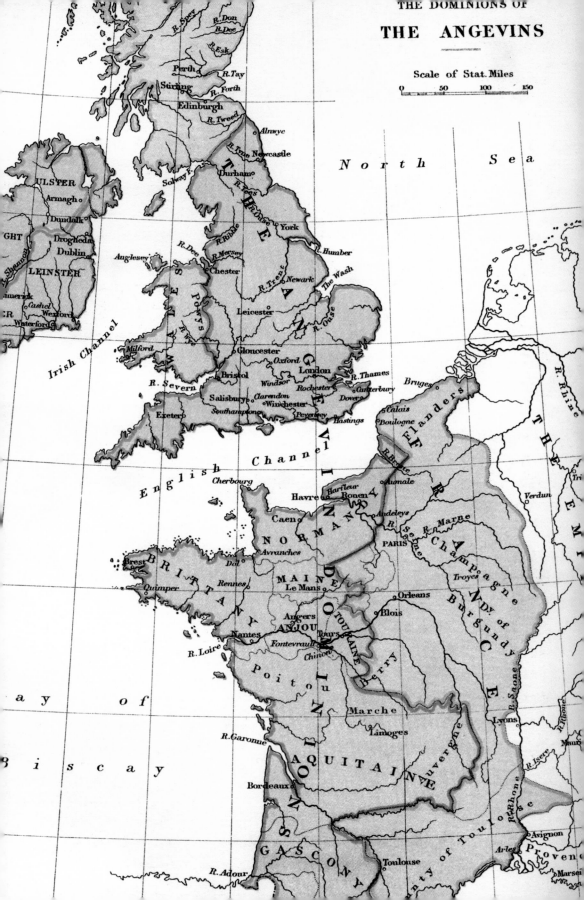

THE DOMINIONS OF
THE ANGEVINS

Scale of Stat. Miles

0   50   100   150

North Sea

R. Spey
R. Don
R. Dee
R. Esk
Perth
R. Tay
Stirling
R. Forth
Edinburgh
R. Tweed
Alnwyc
R. Tyne   Newcastle
Durham
ULSTER
Armagh
Dundalk
Solway F.
R. Tees
Drogheda
Dublin
York
LEINSTER
R. Dee
R. Ribble
R. Mersey
Anglesey
Chester
R. Humber
R. Trent
Newark
Shannon
Cashel
Wexford
Waterford
Milford
R. Severn
R. Wye
Leicester
The Wash
R. Ouse
Gloucester
Oxford
Bristol
London
R. Thames
Windsor
Rochester
Canterbury
Salisbury
Clarendon
Dover
Exeter
Southampton
Winchester
Pevensey
Hastings
Bruges

Irish Channel

WALES
POWYS
THE ANGEVIN

English Channel

Calais
Boulogne
Flanders
THE EMP

Cherbourg
Havre
Barfleur
Rouen
Aumale
Verdun
Caen
Andeleys
R. Seine
NORMANDY
Avranches
R. Marne
PARIS
Champagne
BRITTANY
Dol
Rennes
MAINE
Le Mans
Troyes
Brest
Quimper
TOURAINE
Orleans
D. OF BURGUNDY
Angers
Tours
Blois
Nantes
ANJOU
Fontevrault
Chinon
R. Loire
Berry
POITOU
Marche
Limoges
R. Garonne
Lyons
R. Saone
AQUITAINE
Auvergne
R. Isere
Bay of Biscay
Bordeaux
R. Rhone
Avignon
Arles
GASCONY
Province
County of Toulouse
Toulouse
R. Adour

North Sea
R. Rhine
Tri

IN ThE ShADOW OF ThE LIONhEART

WHEN Richard became King of England in 1189, John found himself next in line to the throne, his other brothers Henry and Geoffrey having died by this time. Richard bestowed John with power and lands: marriage to the rich heiress Isabella of Gloucester; the counties of Nottingham, Derby Dorset, Somerset, Cornwall and Devon; and he was made Count of Mortain in Normandy. But this was not enough for him. When Richard departed on the Third Crusade in 1190, John began plotting to take the English throne with the help of the French king, Philip Augustus. John had a great stroke of luck when Richard, on his return journey from the Holy Land, was shipwrecked and then captured in Germany by the Holy Roman Emperor, Henry VI. Henry wanted a large ransom to free his prisoner; John offered Henry money to keep him incarcerated.

England, loyal to their king, paid the ransom and Richard returned in 1194 to easily quell John's attempted coup against him. When John knelt shaking before Richard seeking forgiveness, the king was dismissively lenient towards him: 'You are only a child.' (He was in his late 20s.) It was a humiliating putdown. Richard expressed his contempt when he told others: 'My brother John is not the man to conquer a country if there is a single person able to make the slightest resistance to his attempts.'

Castle Dürnstein in the Danube valley, Austria; one of the places where Richard I was held captive in 1192.

John was forever in Richard's shadow. Richard was respected and even loved by his subjects and his men. He had earned a reputation for generosity and, most of all, bravery; as a knight fighting in France and as a renowned crusader fighting in the Holy Land, Richard was famous for his glorious deeds across the known world. His fame was further spread when troubadours sang songs about him. He was everything that his brother was not, and John could never compete with him.

In the immediate aftermath of his failed rebellion, John attempted to reassure his brother of his newfound loyalty. He quickly went to Évreux in Normandy and took the castle there. Its garrison did not know of his reconciliation with Richard: they thought he was still allied with King Philip of France. John massacred them. One report from the time claims he put their heads on poles.

Even before he was king, John had earned himself a reputation for treachery. This reputation was to darken even further when, with the unexpected death of Richard I from a crossbow wound in April 1199, John ascended to the throne of England.

Statue of Richard I outside the Houses of Parliament.

Richard I (the Lionheart) arrives at Acre during the Third Crusade, 1191.

SUCCESSFUL FIRST YEARS AS KING

J OHN'S reign started well with a successful show of force as he progressed with a large army across his lands in France. In May 1200 at Le Goulet he secured the peace treaty he wished for with King Philip of France. By this treaty he was acknowledging, as King Henry II and King Richard I had before him, Philip's overlordship of English territories in France. However, the difference this time was that John agreed to pay the huge relief (monetary transaction) of 20,000 marks to Philip in order that the French monarch would recognise John as Richard I's heir to these fiefs. By contrast, Henry II and Richard I had never handed over any money. Between the peace treaty and the financial sum involved, John quickly earned for himself a disparaging new nickname: 'Softsword'.

King John's reign began successfully, but it was to go disastrously wrong.

Trouble soon flared elsewhere in France. John had his first marriage to Isabella of Gloucester annulled and in August 1200 married Isabella of Angoulême, who was barely 12 years of age. Chronicles attributed the move to John's unhealthy lusts; in fact, John was cleverly ensuring that the marriage would bring him lands in a vitally strategic area. But Isabella had already been betrothed to a powerful local baron, Hugh the Brown, Lord of Lusignan. All might have been well had John suitably compensated Hugh's loss of face with money and rewards; instead he acted spitefully and insensitively. He thereby earned the enmity of the Lusignans. They were soon to seek their revenge.

John achieved even greater success in 1202. War broke out with France again and King Philip supported the 16-year-old Arthur of Brittany against John. Arthur was John's nephew, the son of John's deceased brother Geoffrey of Brittany. For many he was the true heir to the English Crown; at one point King Richard I had even named him as such. That summer Arthur, with the support of French and Lusignan troops, besieged John's 80-year-old mother Eleanor of Aquitaine in the Castle of Mirebeau. John made a rapid forced march there and surprised the enemy while they were eating pigeon for breakfast. He defeated the opposing forces decisively. It was a huge victory, which saw him capture his leading foes. He wrote home elatedly that he 'had got the lot'. The greatest prize was the contender to his throne, Arthur. John's reign had had a good start.

Isabella of Angoulême, King John's young bride.

Arthur of Brittany, John's nephew, pays homage to the French king, Philip Augustus.

MISTREATMENT
AND MURDER

A prisoner of King John may have suffered in this way.

A depiction of the murder of Arthur of Brittany, at Rouen in 1203, allegedly on the orders of King John.

AT this moment of supreme triumph, John's success was marred by his vindictive treatment of his prisoners. He held many of the knights in extremely poor conditions. Those placed in Corfe Castle rioted and refused to surrender; it is reported that some of them preferred to starve to death rather than surrender to John again. A consequence was that John alienated the prisoners' relatives, many of whom were powerful lords in Normandy. In so doing, he pushed some of them into the French camp so that, when he later needed their help, it was not forthcoming.

Worse still were the rumours that John had murdered his nephew while held in prison. We do not know for certain of Arthur's exact fate, but it is clear that something terrible befell him while in John's custody. Chronicles variously tell that John had stabbed him in a drunken rage and dumped his body in the River Seine, or that he died after being castrated. Arthur was never seen again. Whatever the truth of the teenager's fate, all were shocked and deemed that John's hands had been tainted by royal blood.

Opposite: Corfe Castle, where captured knights rioted against King John's harsh regime.

10

COLLAPSE OF THE EMPIRE

KING Philip of France allied with the enemies John had created. With Breton and Lusignan troops, and with the connivance of lords who owed allegiance to King John, Philip began a full-scale invasion of the Duchy of Normandy. John was sluggish in his efforts to resist the attack. He launched a couple of half-hearted military operations but, in a telling lack of leadership, he secretly deserted Normandy in December 1203, leaving his army to continue the fight without him. He was never to return.

The great set-piece of the war was the epic six-month siege of John's Château-Gaillard that began in September 1203. When an English relief-force failed to lift the French siege, John fell into deeper inaction. Hundreds of non-combatants were expelled from Château-Gaillard; many starved to death in the no-man's-land between the castle and the French lines. In March the fortress was stormed and taken. Philip was then able to move on to Rouen and tell its citizens that John had deserted them and that they should change

A 14th-century illustration of the Siege of Château-Gaillard in 1204.

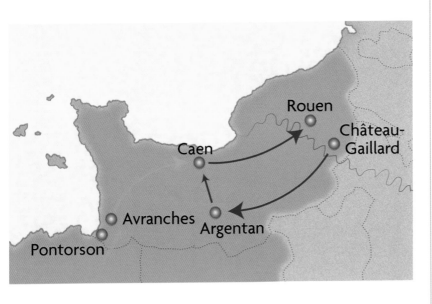

King Philip's successful invasion of Normandy in 1204. The dark blue arrows indicate the movement of Philip's forces; the light blue the movement of Philip's Breton allies.

their allegiance to him as their lord; if they did not, he would hang them. They submitted and Normandy became French.

The chronicler Roger of Wendover claims that, during this time, John was more interested in staying in bed with his young bride than in defending Normandy, and that John nonchalantly said that whatever the King of France took from him now, 'I will one day recover'.

Philip continued with his successful momentum and invaded Anjou, John's ancestral homeland. It quickly succumbed. One major reason for this, apart from John's conspicuous absence, was that John had alienated his powerful

King Philip Augustus of France from the 13th-century manuscript *Grandes Chroniques de France A Royal History of France.*

seneschal there, William des Roches, who had followed other lords over to the French side. Large parts of Poitou were also taken. John had suffered a comprehensive and catastrophic defeat. The Angevin Empire had crumbled.

John planned a massive campaign to regain his lands in 1205, but this was called off when his barons, smarting at John's oppressive financial regime, refused to go. John personally led a major expeditionary force to southern France in 1206, but this had the limited objective of preserving his lands in Gascony, not regaining what he had lost. He agreed a two-year truce with Philip and returned to England where he made further plans.

He would spend the rest of his reign trying to win back his lands in France, and it was the ruthless pursuit of this end that led to Magna Carta.

JOhN AND ThE ChuRCh:
INTERDICT AND EXCOMMUNICATION

A baptism scene: baptism was still allowed in England during the interdict.

J OHN was quickly embroiled in a new struggle: this time with the Church. John's moral behaviour was rarely exemplary, but he displayed a reasonably conventional piety when it came to matters of faith. Although he made numerous, generous donations to the poor and to religious houses, he wanted to keep the rich and powerful Church in England under tight control.

When Hubert Walter, Archbishop of Canterbury, died in 1205, John lined up for the job his trusted advisor, John de Gray, Bishop of Norwich. But the Pope wanted another candidate: Cardinal Stephen Langton. Pope Innocent III was a headstrong pontiff who had grand ideas about asserting the power of the Church over monarchs, particularly in this case. John refused to accept Langton and a bitter diplomatic conflict ensued between the King of England and the Pope. It was to last until 1213.

John had good reasons for not wanting Langton: he had spent years as a scholar in Paris and was close to the French royal court there; furthermore, his brother Simon was among the discontented barons in England. John played for time but Innocent grew impatient and placed the whole of England under a papal interdict in 1208. This meant that all church services and sacraments, with the exceptions of baptism and extreme unction, were suspended across the land. Bodies were buried in the woods, ditches and by the side of the road. Only two bishops remained in all of England. The following year, the Pope excommunicated John from the Church.

John raked in money during the interdict, exploiting the weakened Church to fill his war chests. He confiscated clerical property and fined the clergy. He even held the mistresses of supposedly celibate clergy for ransom, releasing them only on payment. Over the period of the interdict he amassed the huge sum of over £65,000 (over £30 million in today's money) from the Church.

But the excommunication encouraged John's enemies at home and abroad even further. King Philip planned a French invasion in 1213 with papal blessing. John wanted the Pope back on his side and so he dramatically submitted to Rome at the last moment. He accepted Langton as Archbishop of Canterbury, promised recompense to the Church and, in a surprise move, placed all his lands under the protection of Innocent III, holding them as fiefs of the Pope. A successful pre-emptive strike by English naval forces against the French fleet harboured at Damme in May 1213 ended Philip's threat. John appeared to be in the ascendant once more.

Pope Innocent III with some Franciscan monks: he quarrelled with King John over who should be Archbishop of Canterbury.

Following a period of interdict, King John finally submits to the papacy, surrendering England to Pope Innocent III and receiving it again as a papal fief.

MASTER OF THE BRITISH ISLES

JOHN was now free to impose his dominance over the British Isles. In 1209, fearing a rebellion in Scotland and Ireland supported by the French, John marched north with a large army. He made the old Scottish King, William the Lion, accept costly and humiliating terms. In 1210 he led a huge force of 800 knights and 1,000 infantry to Ireland where William Marshal and other powerful lords, such as William de Braose and the de Lacy brothers, had been in open rebellion against him. They were protesting at John's financial and political demands in search of funds for campaigning in France. The barons submitted or fled. In Wales, Llywelyn the Great also rebelled, but faced by John in 1211 he retreated to Snowdonia and agreed to harsh terms. The Barnwell annalist observed: 'In Ireland, Scotland and Wales there was no one who did not bow to the nod of the King of England.'

The effigy of William Marshal, perhaps the world's most famous knight.

John also crushed a personal enemy. For years William de Braose had been one of John's right-hand men. He was Lord of Bamber and Barnstaple, and a marcher lord in South Wales. In 1201 John offered him the honour of Limerick in Ireland for 5,000 marks. Six years later, de Braose still owed the bulk of this money. John, ever mistrustful of his great magnates, also suspected him of allying with William Marshal. In 1210 John went after him. De Braose escaped to France, but his lands, his wife Matilda and his son fell into John's hands. In perhaps his most malicious and notorious act, John let them starve to death in Windsor Castle. One chronicler reports that their bodies were found with the mother slumped between her son's legs with her head lying on his chest; she had been gnawing at his cheeks for food. Rumours also circulated that John had killed them because de Braose and his wife knew the truth about what happened to Arthur of Brittany: de Braose had been with John at the time of the teenager's disappearance.

The statue of Llywelyn the Great in Conwy, Wales. Llywelyn was ground into submission by King John in 1211. However, he did not stay defeated for long and he went on to become de facto ruler of Wales.

One historian has called the act 'the greatest mistake John made during his reign'. The barons of England were once more shocked by John's vicious behaviour. If even the de Braose family could be persecuted in this cruel way, then none of them could feel safe. They decided it was time to act.

Windsor Castle, where William de Braose's wife and son starved to death in 1210.

THε GRIεVΛNCεS OF THε BΛRONS

IN the late summer of 1212 John mustered a large army to march into Wales and quell another rebellion. As he sat down to dinner on the eve of his campaign – after having hung 28 Welsh hostages, one a 7-year-old boy – a messenger informed him of a baronial plot to dethrone him, either by abandoning him to the Welsh or by killing him while in Wales. John took fright and immediately called off the expedition.

The aggrieved barons under King John, shown in much later armour.

Resentment against John had been growing for years. Not only did many of his barons not feel safe after the de Braose affair, but they were heartily sick of the financial burdens that John was increasingly imposing on them. Much has been made of John's proficiency in collecting revenues from the country. He personally oversaw the effective machinery of government, always keeping a close eye on the Exchequer. He reformed the bureaucracy, ensuring that judicial and administrative records were assiduously gathered; he also overhauled the court system and standardised weights. But being a good king required more than efficient bookkeeping. His administrative success was counterproductive, for it antagonised his barons ever further.

The payment of taxes in the 13th century. King John's high taxes formed part of the reason why his barons rebelled against him and forced him to seal Magna Carta.

The barons were especially unhappy about certain financial instruments. One was 'scutage'. This was money paid in lieu of military service, which the king then used to hire mercenaries. The barons were reluctant to join John's armies in France: not only was it expensive for them but they had little faith in him achieving victories from which the spoils of war would recompense them for their financial outlays. Many barons, such as Robert Fitzwalter and Roger Bigod, expressed their discontent about scutage as far back as 1205; more were to do so in 1212 and 1213. In 1214 the scutage rate hit a record high. There were also more of them being levied than ever before.

A 15th-century depiction of a magistrate being bribed. Corruption was widespread during King John's reign.

Another issue, reflecting the king's unsettling and increasingly arbitrary nature of rule, was the amercement penalty system. Many people had to pay heavy cash fines for misdemeanours such as neglect of public duties. Thus when Robert de Ros, Sheriff of Cumberland, failed to keep some prisoners in custody he was fined 300 marks. The fines could be very steep. William of Cornborough died in gaol because he was unable to pay his. Ordinary people were also charged regularly and often unfairly, with the minimum fine commonly amounting to over 20 per cent of a labourer's annual wage. Men were compelled to buy the goodwill of the king, even if they had done nothing wrong.

It was widely felt that John was corrupting the justice system and manipulating it for his own ends in order to generate more revenue for the Crown. Scutages, amercements and justice were all criticized by his barons.

Lady Justice: she holds the scales of justice in one hand to indicate that each side will be heard fairly in a court of law; and a sword in the other to represent enforcement and the power of reason.

John was not averse to making money by blackmailing his barons. Official government records reveal that Robert de Vaux offered John 750 marks and five high-quality horses in order that the king 'would keep quiet about the wife of Henry Pinel'.

There were personal grievances, too, as John was a notorious womaniser, taking as mistresses and conquests the wives and daughters of some powerful men. Other kings had done this, but none so insensitively as John. Government records state that 'the wife of Hugh de Neville offers the king 200 chickens so that she may lie one night with her husband'. Hugh, a leading royal official, later joined the rebellious barons. The leading rebel barons Eustace de Vesci and Robert Fitzwalter swallowed their pride to accuse John of forcing himself on their wives and daughters. Anonymous of Béthune, whose own lord fought on John's side, observed that John 'lusted after beautiful women and because of this he ashamed many of the great men of the land, for which he was much hated'.

The final straw came in 1214. At last, John's onerous financial impositions had amassed so huge a fortune that he could launch his long-awaited attack on France to regain his lands there. It was a massive operation. His German allies (whom he had expensively bankrolled) invaded France from the Lowlands in the north-east, while John led his army from the west. But at the close-run Battle of Bouvines in July, King Philip decisively defeated John's allies. John's part was equally ignominious: a little earlier at La Roche-aux-Moines he had turned around and fled at the approach of a French army. Once more, he had squandered the treasure he had so painfully extracted from his people.

John still did not learn his lesson. He returned to England in October demanding scutage payments. The barons had had enough.

King John took for himself the wives and daughters of other powerful men.

The Battle of Bouvines, 27 July 1214. This was the final blow for John. His defeat here led to the English barons taking decisive action against him.

MAGNA CARTA

E ARLY in May 1215, the discontented barons broke their homage to John and formed the Army of God and the Holy Church. It was a declaration of war on their king. Among their leaders were Robert Fitzwalter the Lord of Dunmow, Roger Bigod the Earl of Norfolk, Geoffrey de Mandeville the Earl of Essex, Saer de Quincey the Earl of Winchester, Henry de Bohun the Earl of Hereford, and other powerful lords. They offered the Crown of England to Prince Louis of France, King Philip's son and heir, if he would come over the Channel with an army to help them. On 17 May the barons seized the capital of London.

Plaster maquette of Stephen Langton by John Thomas (sculptor). This is one of 17 maquettes for life-sized bronzes representing the signatories of Magna Carta. The bronze can be seen in the Canterbury Heritage Museum.

The rebels drew up their demands in a document known as the Articles of the Barons; it was, in effect, the first draft of what was later to be known as the Great Charter, or Magna Carta. Now facing huge threats, John agreed to meet the rebels. By 10 June the king's men and advisers were in talks with the barons at Runnymede on the River Thames. One chronicler reports that 'nearly all the nobility of England' were there – an indication of how all understood the importance of what was unfolding.

When John first heard their demands, Roger of Wendover claims he sarcastically snarled: 'Why do these barons not just ask for my kingdom?' But he had little choice. The king had to accept the Articles of the Barons if he were to re-establish peace and fend off a French invasion. The document, drawn up under the guidance of John's unwanted Archbishop of Canterbury, Stephen Langton, began with the words: 'These are the articles that the barons seek and the king concedes.' On 15 June John formally agreed to the terms and the king's seal was attached to the document. By 19 June final revisions had been made and the Articles became law as the Charter of Liberties.

This Charter was largely preoccupied with financial matters relating to feudal payments and their regulation concerning inheritance, widows and minors. Money and economic matters featured largely throughout: a number of clauses dealt with debts, tariffs,

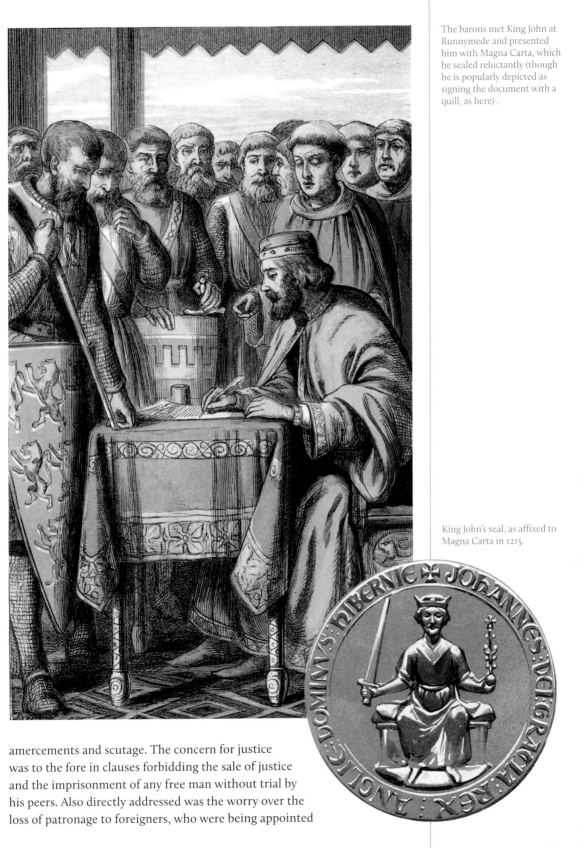

King John's seal, as affixed to Magna Carta in 1215.

amercements and scutage. The concern for justice was to the fore in clauses forbidding the sale of justice and the imprisonment of any free man without trial by his peers. Also directly addressed was the worry over the loss of patronage to foreigners, who were being appointed

leading positions to the detriment of English barons.
The unsettled times are reflected in clauses calling for
the release of hostages, the return of castles and the
removal 'from the kingdom [of] all the foreign knights,
crossbowmen, sergeants and mercenaries that have come
to it, to its harm, with horses and arms'.

The document was designed to maximise its broad appeal
among the barons and to unite as many of them as possible against
John's autocratic and capricious government. The most radical and
remarkable demand of all was the 'security clause', number 61. By this, the
barons presented themselves as acting for 'the community of the realm' and,
through their committee of 25 leading barons, they were to ensure, by force if
necessary, that the king adhered to this agreement.

The Charter was reissued on a number of occasions after 1215 with
amendments, including the removal of the radical security clause: the 1217
reissue, for example, removed the forest clauses, which became part of a
separate Charter, and the 1225 reissue became the more enduring version.

King John had yielded huge swathes of his power as monarch. One
historian has judged the submission to be 'the most fantastic surrender
of any English king to his subjects'. John knew it. The chronicler Matthew
Paris documents that afterwards, 'he gnashed his teeth, rolled his eyes,

caught up sticks and straws and gnawed them like a madman, or tore them to shreds with his fingers'.

The Charter was never going to create immediate peace. In 1215 it simply halted the ongoing war between the king and his rebellious barons. Before long both sides were accusing the other of ill-faith and of breaking the agreement. The barons plundered royal lands and held on to London, while John was deliberately slow in returning lands and castles to them. In August Pope Innocent III annulled the Charter, having been John's ally and overlord since John had submitted to him to end the interdict. It made little difference to the increasing hostilities, however. In October, full-scale war broke out.

Rebel fighters under the command of William d'Albini seized Rochester Castle in Kent. John amassed his forces and laid siege to them. Five siege engines bombarded the walls with stones. John gave an order for 40 pigs to be dispatched to the siege: the fat from them was to assist the firing of the wooden supports of the tunnel excavated to bring the castle's walls down. When mining collapsed a tower, the garrison surrendered and the epic two-month siege was over. John wanted to hang all the rebels but was talked out of this by one of his captains.

It was a good victory. But the French were about to invade.

John's fury at the sealing of Magna Carta.

'A PILLAGER OF HIS OWN PEOPLE'

O VER the Christmas period of 1215/16, John took the war across the country. In a rapid march from St Albans he headed north, leaving a trail of smoke in his wake. In January he sacked Berwick with great violence. He swept away all before him and seemed to be victorious. He was trying to crush all resistance against him before the French arrived, but it came at a cost. The king had inflicted huge destruction and misery not only on his enemies but also on his own people. Ralph of Coggeshall reports John's men being 'dedicated to plunder and burning' and that John was 'the merciless one'. Roger of Wendover confirms the extent of the devastation caused by John's army:

> Running about with swords and knives drawn, the soldiers ransacked towns, houses, cemeteries and churches, robbing everyone, and sparing neither women nor children. The wretched creatures uttered pitiable cries and dreadful groans, but there was no one to show them pity, for their torturers were satisfied with nothing but their money.

The mistreatment by King John of his own people during the war of 1216.

John was literally, as the Barnwell annalist had said, 'a pillager of his
own people'.

In May 1216 Prince Louis invaded with a powerful force. John led an army
to oppose his landing at Thanet. Chroniclers report that the king 'little
emboldened his men and little comforted them' and, fearing desertion by his
own troops over to Louis, 'he chose to
retreat rather than engage in battle'.
John had the chance to fight Louis
on the shore and prevent him from
gaining a foothold, but once again he
backed away from direct combat.

The territory in England
taken by Prince Louis during
his invasion of May 1216 to
September 1217.

Louis joined up with the disgruntled
barons in London. Up to two-
thirds of the baronage in England
paid allegiance to him as their new
monarch, King Louis I of England.
King Alexander II of Scotland was able
to march all the way to Dover to meet
with Louis as one king to another. The
French occupied and ruled over one-
third of England, from Lincoln in the
north to the Isle of Wight in the south.
The only isolated points of resistance
within this occupied territory were the
powerful castles of Windsor and Dover,
both of which were besieged. John
retreated to the west of the country
where he planned how he might recoup
his losses and drive the French from his
kingdom. He had already lost most of
his lands in France; now he had lost a
third of England.

THE LAST DISASTER

'HIS CHEST EITHER HAD TO BURST OR
TO VOMIT ITS VENOM SOMEWHERE.'
Richard of Devizes

JOHN spent the rest of his reign trying, unsuccessfully, to regain control of his kingdom. After a period of defensive withdrawal, which he spent regrouping, he attempted in the autumn to win back the initiative with a ravaging campaign that demonstrated one of his occasional periods of furious activity. This included the burning of Crowland Abbey, where one chronicler depicts him setting alight the harvest fields and running through the black smoke and flames like a deranged demon. He had lost none of his ability to strike fear into the hearts of his enemies: 'They fled before his face, dreading his presence as if it were lightning.'

King John loses his treasure, clothing and provisions while crossing The Wash. He subsequently contracts dysentery.

At Lynn in October (now King's Lynn), however, he fell ill. This may have been dysentery, but Ralph of Coggeshall blames it on the king's gluttony during a feast. John tried to continue his campaign and, on 11 October, he led his army in a short cut across The Wash at low tide. John's haste backfired. Whether due to the tide catching the column unaware, or the treacherous quicksand that exists there, his baggage train and treasure were reported to have been lost beneath the waves (some of it may actually have been stolen after John's death). Roger of Wendover reports John's 'anguish of mind over his possessions swallowed up by the water'. It was the last disaster of a disastrous reign.

John's health quickly deteriorated, especially after he heard the news that his castle at Dover had arranged a truce with the French. He knew his time was nearly up and made his will. In great pain, he was dragged on a litter to Newark Castle, 'moaning and groaning' that the journey was killing him. When he arrived at his final destination, he confessed his sins and received Communion for the last time. On the night of 18/19 October 1216 he died in the middle of a great storm.

The king's heart was cut out and taken to Croxton Abbey, while his body was buried in Worcester Cathedral. Few tears were shed for him on his death.

Newark Castle on the banks of the River Trent in Nottinghamshire, where King John died in October 1216.

The tomb of King John in Worcester Cathedral.

LEGACY

ITH John dead, and his 9-year-old son Henry III as king, it was left to others to defeat the French and drive them out of England the following year. The country took years to recover from the costs of the baronial rebellion and French invasion.

John's reign as King of England was a failure. In recent years, some historians have tried to paint a more positive picture of John, but this is hard to do when one recalls his deeds as monarch: the murder of his young nephew; the English lands lost in France; the starvation of a mother and her son; the submission of his kingdom as a fief to the papacy; his blatant adultery; his cowardly retreat from combat; the taxation that finally pushed the country into open rebellion; and his death with London and one-third of the country under French rule. If we turn to the words of John's contemporaries, the message is clear. Anonymous of Béthune said of him: 'He was a very wicked man; he was cruel to all men.' And for the chronicler Matthew Paris there were certainly no redeeming features: 'Foul as Hell is, Hell itself is defiled by the presence of John.'

'Foul as Hell is, Hell itself is defiled by the presence of John.' A carving from the 13th-century Abbey Church of St Foy in France shows the tortures and punishments of Hell.

Yet from John's reign came the greatest of legacies – Magna Carta. It had been forced upon him as a damning verdict of his rule, but it has endured as a global symbol of political rights and freedom. After 1215 the Charter was reissued several times, remaining prominent throughout the 13th century. The 1217 reissue removed the forest clauses and put them instead into the Charter of Forest Liberties, and by 1225 there were only 37 clauses. After the Middle Ages, the influence of Magna Carta declined – it is not even mentioned in Shakespeare's *The Life and Death of King John* – but during King Charles I's reign and the period of the English Civil War it was once again invoked to defend the rights of individuals against what they saw as the growing despotism of an overbearing monarch.

American history has also ensured its ongoing importance. Before and during the American War of Independence, Magna Carta provided the colonists with an intellectual and constitutional rallying cry against what many deemed to be the tyranny of kings. The seal of the state of Massachusetts, designed by Paul Revere in 1775, depicts a militiaman with a sword in one hand and a copy of Magna Carta in the other. The 1791 Bill of Rights directly echoes clause 39 of the 1215 Charter in its proclamation that no person shall be 'deprived of life, liberty, or property, without due process of law'.

In short, the fundamental principles of Magna Carta remain in law today, and are adhered to all over the world. The tyrannical reign of Bad King John was certainly more influential than many may think.

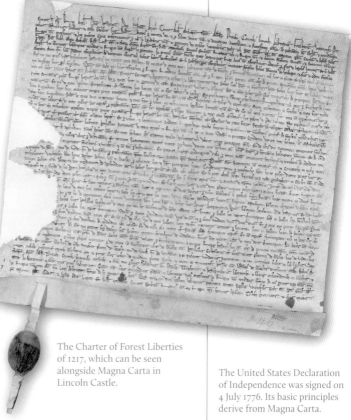

The Charter of Forest Liberties of 1217, which can be seen alongside Magna Carta in Lincoln Castle.

The United States Declaration of Independence was signed on 4 July 1776. Its basic principles derive from Magna Carta.

PLACES TO VISIT

Dover Castle, one of the only fortifications within the territory taken by Prince Louis to remain loyal to King John.

Corfe Castle
www.corfe-castle.co.uk

Dover Castle
www.english-heritage.org.uk/
daysout/properties/dover-castle

Hereford Cathedral
www.herefordcathedral.org

Lincoln Castle
www.lincolnshire.gov.uk/visiting/historic-buildings/lincoln-castle

Newark Castle
www.newark-sherwooddc.gov.uk/newarkcastle

Rochester Castle
www.english-heritage.org.uk/daysout/properties/rochester-castle

Runnymede
www.nationaltrust.org.uk/runnymede

Lincoln Castle, the East Gate, where a surviving Magna Carta from 1215 is on display.

Salisbury Cathedral
www.salisburycathedral.org.uk

Temple Church
www.templechurch.com

Tower of London
www.hrp.org.uk/TowerOfLondon

Windsor Castle
www.windsor.gov.uk/things-to-do/
windsor-castle

The Tower of London, first established by William the Conqueror in 1066. It was expanded by Henry III, King John's son.

Worcester Cathedral
www.worcestercathedral.co.uk